This journal belongs to:

_____

MY
READING
LIFE

MY
READING
LIFE

What I Read, How It Felt,
and What I Thought

SPRUCE BOOKS
A Sasquatch Books Imprint
sasquatchbooks.com

Why Keep a Reading Journal?

"I have forgotten the books I have read, and so I have the dinners I have eaten; but they both helped make me."

—Anonymous

Book lovers do not need to be reminded of the pleasures of reading—the power of books to transport us to lands unknown or imagined or, conversely, to make us see familiar places with a fresh eye; the way books drop us into the lives, minds, and hearts of other people so thoroughly that we become those characters, at least for the time we are reading; the incomparable feeling when we finish a great book, knowing that reading it has made us into a different person than we were before we opened it.

Book lovers sometimes do need to be reminded, however, of the title of that book that so transported us or the name of that author whose book was so brilliant that we really have to share it with someone special. This journal is designed to for that book lover.

Our reading lives offer such profound pleasures; keeping a journal is a wonderful way to deepen and enhance them. This journal offers readers the opportunity to write down the reasons why a book saved your life, or made you ugly cry, or caused you to snort with laughter; to make a note of a book you know is the perfect gift for a dear friend or that you want to suggest for your next book-club meeting; to make lists of the authors you love; to jot down a striking phrase or passage that you want to remember. These are just a few of the joys of reading that are enhanced by the act of keeping a journal.

Of course, journaling has many benefits beyond its obvious function of helping us keep track of our thoughts—it supports us in being mindful, focuses our attention, and helps us to process our feelings. Science has plenty to say on this point, with many studies offering evidence that keeping a journal is a positive wellness practice that improves our sense of well-being, sharpens our memories, reduces our feelings of anxiety, and can even help lift us out of depression. Book lovers know that beyond the wellness benefits of a reading journal lies the satisfaction of being able to look back and remember what made each book special.

This journal is designed with all of that in mind, but also specifically to be a chronicle of your reading life, to enrich your experience of reading not only by keeping track of the books you've read but by giving you the opportunity to delve deeper into the feelings and thoughts you experience while reading.

Inside you'll find plenty of log pages you can jot down just the basics like the title and author or share your thoughts on plot and character, and your notes on what worked for you, from the cover to the ending—it's up to you. Interspersed among the log pages are list pages for noting everything you want to remember, from genres to authors, gift-giving notes to future-read lists, and even your favorite bookstores.

Really engaging with a book can be immersive and transformative. Writing about what you felt, even if it's just to jot down a few impressions, allows you to take away something more tangible from that experience.

For true book lovers, though there may be nothing better than reading a good book, recalling what you loved about it comes in a close second. So use this book in whatever way works for you, as a place to make lists of your favorites, as a repository for your feelings, or simply as a log of your reading life during a certain period. Each time you look through it, you'll have the pleasure of being reminded of what you gained from the books you've read.

TITLE . . . .

AUTHOR . . . .

DATE READ . . . .

THE COVER

RATING   1   2   3   4   5

WHAT DREW ME TO THIS COVER/ WHAT I DIDN'T LOVE ABOUT THIS COVER

. . . .

. . . .

. . . .

WHY I CHOSE THIS BOOK . . . .

. . . .

OTHER BOOKS I HAVE READ OR PLAN TO READ BY THIS AUTHOR
(Check if read already)

◯ . . . .

◯ . . . .

◯ . . . .

◯ . . . .

THE FEELING(S) THIS BOOK EVOKED IN ME . . . .

. . . .

FAVORITE PASSAGE(S) . . . .
. . . .
. . . .
. . . .
. . . .
. . . .
. . . .

DID READING THIS BOOK CHANGE ME IN ANY WAY? . . . .
. . . .
. . . .

WHO WOULD I LIKE TO SHARE THIS BOOK WITH?
WHAT WOULD I HOPE FOR THEM TO TAKE AWAY FROM IT?
. . . .
. . . .

NOT RECOMMENDED? WHY? . . . .

REREAD?   Y   N

RATINGS

WRITING STYLE	Loved it	Just okay	Didn't enjoy
MESSAGE	Loved it	Just okay	Didn't enjoy
READING EXPERIENCE	Loved it	Just okay	Didn't enjoy

TITLE . . . .

AUTHOR . . . .

DATE READ . . . .

THE COVER

RATING   1   2   3   4   5

WHAT DREW ME TO THIS COVER/ WHAT I DIDN'T LOVE ABOUT THIS COVER

. . . .

. . . .

. . . .

WHY I CHOSE THIS BOOK . . . .

. . . .

OTHER BOOKS I HAVE READ OR PLAN TO READ BY THIS AUTHOR
(Check if read already)

◯ . . . .

◯ . . . .

◯ . . . .

◯ . . . .

THE FEELING(S) THIS BOOK EVOKED IN ME . . . .

. . . .

FAVORITE PASSAGE(S) . . . .

. . . .

. . . .

. . . .

. . . .

. . . .

. . . .

DID READING THIS BOOK CHANGE ME IN ANY WAY? . . . .

. . . .

. . . .

WHO WOULD I LIKE TO SHARE THIS BOOK WITH?
WHAT WOULD I HOPE FOR THEM TO TAKE AWAY FROM IT?

. . . .

. . . .

NOT RECOMMENDED? WHY? . . . .

REREAD?   Y   N

RATINGS

WRITING STYLE	Loved it	Just okay	Didn't enjoy
MESSAGE	Loved it	Just okay	Didn't enjoy
READING EXPERIENCE	Loved it	Just okay	Didn't enjoy

TITLE . . . .

AUTHOR . . . .

DATE READ . . . .

THE COVER

RATING   1   2   3   4   5

WHAT DREW ME TO THIS COVER/ WHAT I DIDN'T LOVE ABOUT THIS COVER

. . . .

. . . .

. . . .

WHY I CHOSE THIS BOOK . . . .

. . . .

OTHER BOOKS I HAVE READ OR PLAN TO READ BY THIS AUTHOR
(Check if read already)

◯ . . . .

◯ . . . .

◯ . . . .

◯ . . . .

THE FEELING(S) THIS BOOK EVOKED IN ME . . . .

. . . .

FAVORITE PASSAGE(S) . . . .

. . . .

. . . .

. . . .

. . . .

. . . .

. . . .

DID READING THIS BOOK CHANGE ME IN ANY WAY? . . . .

. . . .

. . . .

WHO WOULD I LIKE TO SHARE THIS BOOK WITH?
WHAT WOULD I HOPE FOR THEM TO TAKE AWAY FROM IT?

. . . .

. . . .

NOT RECOMMENDED? WHY? . . . .

REREAD?   Y   N

RATINGS

WRITING STYLE	Loved it	Just okay	Didn't enjoy
MESSAGE	Loved it	Just okay	Didn't enjoy
READING EXPERIENCE	Loved it	Just okay	Didn't enjoy

TITLE . . . .

AUTHOR . . . .

DATE READ . . . .

THE COVER

RATING   1   2   3   4   5

WHAT DREW ME TO THIS COVER/ WHAT I DIDN'T LOVE ABOUT THIS COVER

. . . .

. . . .

. . . .

WHY I CHOSE THIS BOOK . . . .

. . . .

OTHER BOOKS I HAVE READ OR PLAN TO READ BY THIS AUTHOR
(Check if read already)

◯ . . . .

◯ . . . .

◯ . . . .

◯ . . . .

THE FEELING(S) THIS BOOK EVOKED IN ME . . . .

. . . .

FAVORITE PASSAGE(S) . . . .

. . . .

. . . .

. . . .

. . . .

. . . .

. . . .

DID READING THIS BOOK CHANGE ME IN ANY WAY? . . . .

. . . .

. . . .

WHO WOULD I LIKE TO SHARE THIS BOOK WITH?
WHAT WOULD I HOPE FOR THEM TO TAKE AWAY FROM IT?

. . . .

. . . .

NOT RECOMMENDED? WHY? . . . .

REREAD?   Y   N

RATINGS

WRITING STYLE	Loved it	Just okay	Didn't enjoy
MESSAGE	Loved it	Just okay	Didn't enjoy
READING EXPERIENCE	Loved it	Just okay	Didn't enjoy

Favorite Authors: Coffee, Dinner, or Drinks?

There are some authors who feel like old friends from the moment you start reading their words. You just know you'd get along. Other authors come as a complete surprise. Which authors would you love to sit down and share a cup of tea or coffee with? Who would you invite to a dinner party? Who would you love to share a few drinks with?

TITLE . . . .

AUTHOR . . . .

DATE READ . . . .

THE COVER

RATING   1   2   3   4   5

WHAT DREW ME TO THIS COVER/ WHAT I DIDN'T LOVE ABOUT THIS COVER

. . . .

. . . .

. . . .

WHY I CHOSE THIS BOOK . . . .

. . . .

OTHER BOOKS I HAVE READ OR PLAN TO READ BY THIS AUTHOR
(Check if read already)

    ◯ . . . .

    ◯ . . . .

    ◯ . . . .

    ◯ . . . .

THE FEELING(S) THIS BOOK EVOKED IN ME . . . .

. . . .

FAVORITE PASSAGE(S) . . . .

. . . .

. . . .

. . . .

. . . .

. . . .

. . . .

DID READING THIS BOOK CHANGE ME IN ANY WAY? . . . .

. . . .

. . . .

WHO WOULD I LIKE TO SHARE THIS BOOK WITH?
WHAT WOULD I HOPE FOR THEM TO TAKE AWAY FROM IT?

. . . .

. . . .

NOT RECOMMENDED? WHY? . . . .

REREAD?   Y   N

RATINGS

WRITING STYLE	Loved it	Just okay	Didn't enjoy
MESSAGE	Loved it	Just okay	Didn't enjoy
READING EXPERIENCE	Loved it	Just okay	Didn't enjoy

TITLE . . . .

AUTHOR . . . .

DATE READ . . . .

THE COVER

RATING   1   2   3   4   5

WHAT DREW ME TO THIS COVER/ WHAT I DIDN'T LOVE ABOUT THIS COVER

. . . .

. . . .

. . . .

WHY I CHOSE THIS BOOK . . . .

. . . .

OTHER BOOKS I HAVE READ OR PLAN TO READ BY THIS AUTHOR
(Check if read already)

◯ . . . .

◯ . . . .

◯ . . . .

◯ . . . .

THE FEELING(S) THIS BOOK EVOKED IN ME . . . .

. . . .

FAVORITE PASSAGE(S) . . . .

. . . .

. . . .

. . . .

. . . .

. . . .

. . . .

DID READING THIS BOOK CHANGE ME IN ANY WAY? . . . .

. . . .

. . . .

WHO WOULD I LIKE TO SHARE THIS BOOK WITH?
WHAT WOULD I HOPE FOR THEM TO TAKE AWAY FROM IT?

. . . .

. . . .

NOT RECOMMENDED? WHY? . . . .

REREAD?   Y   N

RATINGS

WRITING STYLE	Loved it	Just okay	Didn't enjoy
MESSAGE	Loved it	Just okay	Didn't enjoy
READING EXPERIENCE	Loved it	Just okay	Didn't enjoy

TITLE . . . .

AUTHOR . . . .

DATE READ . . . .

THE COVER

RATING   1   2   3   4   5

WHAT DREW ME TO THIS COVER/ WHAT I DIDN'T LOVE ABOUT THIS COVER

. . . .

. . . .

. . . .

WHY I CHOSE THIS BOOK . . . .

. . . .

OTHER BOOKS I HAVE READ OR PLAN TO READ BY THIS AUTHOR
(Check if read already)

◯ . . . .

◯ . . . .

◯ . . . .

◯ . . . .

THE FEELING(S) THIS BOOK EVOKED IN ME . . . .

. . . .

FAVORITE PASSAGE(S) . . . .

. . . .

. . . .

. . . .

. . . .

. . . .

. . . .

DID READING THIS BOOK CHANGE ME IN ANY WAY? . . . .

. . . .

. . . .

WHO WOULD I LIKE TO SHARE THIS BOOK WITH?
WHAT WOULD I HOPE FOR THEM TO TAKE AWAY FROM IT?

. . . .

. . . .

NOT RECOMMENDED? WHY? . . . .

REREAD?   Y   N

RATINGS

WRITING STYLE	Loved it	Just okay	Didn't enjoy
MESSAGE	Loved it	Just okay	Didn't enjoy
READING EXPERIENCE	Loved it	Just okay	Didn't enjoy

TITLE . . . .

AUTHOR . . . .

DATE READ . . . .

THE COVER

RATING   1   2   3   4   5

WHAT DREW ME TO THIS COVER/ WHAT I DIDN'T LOVE ABOUT THIS COVER

. . . .

. . . .

. . . .

WHY I CHOSE THIS BOOK . . . .

. . . .

OTHER BOOKS I HAVE READ OR PLAN TO READ BY THIS AUTHOR
(Check if read already)

◯ . . . .

◯ . . . .

◯ . . . .

◯ . . . .

THE FEELING(S) THIS BOOK EVOKED IN ME . . . .

. . . .

FAVORITE PASSAGE(S) . . . .

. . . .

. . . .

. . . .

. . . .

. . . .

. . . .

DID READING THIS BOOK CHANGE ME IN ANY WAY? . . . .

. . . .

. . . .

WHO WOULD I LIKE TO SHARE THIS BOOK WITH?
WHAT WOULD I HOPE FOR THEM TO TAKE AWAY FROM IT?

. . . .

. . . .

NOT RECOMMENDED? WHY? . . . .

REREAD?   Y   N

RATINGS

WRITING STYLE	Loved it	Just okay	Didn't enjoy
MESSAGE	Loved it	Just okay	Didn't enjoy
READING EXPERIENCE	Loved it	Just okay	Didn't enjoy

Genre Hound: Mystery

There's something both chilling and comforting about a good mystery novel. The combination is irresistible, whether you're looking for a cozy solution or journey into darkness. My favorite mysteries:

_____

_____

_____

_____

_____

_____

_____

_____

_____

_____

_____

_____

_____

_____

_____

_____

_____

_____

TITLE . . . .

AUTHOR . . . .

DATE READ . . . .

THE COVER

RATING   1   2   3   4   5

WHAT DREW ME TO THIS COVER/ WHAT I DIDN'T LOVE ABOUT THIS COVER

. . . .

. . . .

. . . .

WHY I CHOSE THIS BOOK . . . .

. . . .

OTHER BOOKS I HAVE READ OR PLAN TO READ BY THIS AUTHOR
(Check if read already)

○ . . . .

○ . . . .

○ . . . .

○ . . . .

THE FEELING(S) THIS BOOK EVOKED IN ME . . . .

. . . .

FAVORITE PASSAGE(S) . . . .

. . . .

. . . .

. . . .

. . . .

. . . .

. . . .

DID READING THIS BOOK CHANGE ME IN ANY WAY? . . . .

. . . .

. . . .

WHO WOULD I LIKE TO SHARE THIS BOOK WITH?
WHAT WOULD I HOPE FOR THEM TO TAKE AWAY FROM IT?

. . . .

. . . .

NOT RECOMMENDED? WHY? . . . .

REREAD?   Y   N

RATINGS

WRITING STYLE	Loved it	Just okay	Didn't enjoy
MESSAGE	Loved it	Just okay	Didn't enjoy
READING EXPERIENCE	Loved it	Just okay	Didn't enjoy

TITLE . . . .

AUTHOR . . . .

DATE READ . . . .

THE COVER

RATING   1   2   3   4   5

WHAT DREW ME TO THIS COVER/ WHAT I DIDN'T LOVE ABOUT THIS COVER

. . . .

. . . .

. . . .

WHY I CHOSE THIS BOOK . . . .

. . . .

OTHER BOOKS I HAVE READ OR PLAN TO READ BY THIS AUTHOR
(Check if read already)

◯ . . . .

◯ . . . .

◯ . . . .

◯ . . . .

THE FEELING(S) THIS BOOK EVOKED IN ME . . . .

. . . .

FAVORITE PASSAGE(S) . . . .

. . . .

. . . .

. . . .

. . . .

. . . .

. . . .

DID READING THIS BOOK CHANGE ME IN ANY WAY? . . . .

. . . .

. . . .

WHO WOULD I LIKE TO SHARE THIS BOOK WITH?
WHAT WOULD I HOPE FOR THEM TO TAKE AWAY FROM IT?

. . . .

. . . .

NOT RECOMMENDED? WHY? . . . .

REREAD?   Y   N

RATINGS

WRITING STYLE	Loved it	Just okay	Didn't enjoy
MESSAGE	Loved it	Just okay	Didn't enjoy
READING EXPERIENCE	Loved it	Just okay	Didn't enjoy

TITLE . . . .

AUTHOR . . . .

DATE READ . . . .

THE COVER

RATING   1   2   3   4   5

WHAT DREW ME TO THIS COVER/ WHAT I DIDN'T LOVE ABOUT THIS COVER

. . . .

. . . .

. . . .

WHY I CHOSE THIS BOOK . . . .

. . . .

OTHER BOOKS I HAVE READ OR PLAN TO READ BY THIS AUTHOR
(Check if read already)

○ . . . .

○ . . . .

○ . . . .

○ . . . .

THE FEELING(S) THIS BOOK EVOKED IN ME . . . .

. . . .

FAVORITE PASSAGE(S) . . . .

. . . .

. . . .

. . . .

. . . .

. . . .

. . . .

DID READING THIS BOOK CHANGE ME IN ANY WAY? . . . .

. . . .

. . . .

WHO WOULD I LIKE TO SHARE THIS BOOK WITH?
WHAT WOULD I HOPE FOR THEM TO TAKE AWAY FROM IT?

. . . .

. . . .

NOT RECOMMENDED? WHY? . . . .

REREAD?   Y   N

RATINGS

WRITING STYLE	Loved it	Just okay	Didn't enjoy
MESSAGE	Loved it	Just okay	Didn't enjoy
READING EXPERIENCE	Loved it	Just okay	Didn't enjoy

TITLE . . . .

AUTHOR . . . .

DATE READ . . . .

THE COVER

RATING   1   2   3   4   5

WHAT DREW ME TO THIS COVER/ WHAT I DIDN'T LOVE ABOUT THIS COVER

. . . .

. . . .

. . . .

WHY I CHOSE THIS BOOK . . . .

. . . .

OTHER BOOKS I HAVE READ OR PLAN TO READ BY THIS AUTHOR
(Check if read already)

◯ . . . .

◯ . . . .

◯ . . . .

◯ . . . .

THE FEELING(S) THIS BOOK EVOKED IN ME . . . .

. . . .

FAVORITE PASSAGE(S) . . . .

. . . .

. . . .

. . . .

. . . .

. . . .

. . . .

DID READING THIS BOOK CHANGE ME IN ANY WAY? . . . .

. . . .

. . . .

WHO WOULD I LIKE TO SHARE THIS BOOK WITH?
WHAT WOULD I HOPE FOR THEM TO TAKE AWAY FROM IT?

. . . .

. . . .

NOT RECOMMENDED? WHY? . . . .

REREAD?   Y   N

RATINGS

WRITING STYLE	Loved it	Just okay	Didn't enjoy
MESSAGE	Loved it	Just okay	Didn't enjoy
READING EXPERIENCE	Loved it	Just okay	Didn't enjoy

Gifts That Keep on Giving

Books make the best gifts! These are the books I would most like to give:

TITLE	TO WHOM?	WHY?

TITLE . . . .

AUTHOR . . . .

DATE READ . . . .

THE COVER

RATING   1   2   3   4   5

WHAT DREW ME TO THIS COVER/ WHAT I DIDN'T LOVE ABOUT THIS COVER

. . . .

. . . .

. . . .

WHY I CHOSE THIS BOOK . . . .

. . . .

OTHER BOOKS I HAVE READ OR PLAN TO READ BY THIS AUTHOR
(Check if read already)

○ . . . .

○ . . . .

○ . . . .

○ . . . .

THE FEELING(S) THIS BOOK EVOKED IN ME . . . .

. . . .

FAVORITE PASSAGE(S) . . . .

. . . .

. . . .

. . . .

. . . .

. . . .

. . . .

DID READING THIS BOOK CHANGE ME IN ANY WAY? . . . .

. . . .

. . . .

WHO WOULD I LIKE TO SHARE THIS BOOK WITH?
WHAT WOULD I HOPE FOR THEM TO TAKE AWAY FROM IT?

. . . .

. . . .

NOT RECOMMENDED? WHY? . . . .

REREAD?   Y   N

RATINGS

WRITING STYLE	Loved it	Just okay	Didn't enjoy
MESSAGE	Loved it	Just okay	Didn't enjoy
READING EXPERIENCE	Loved it	Just okay	Didn't enjoy

TITLE. . . . .

AUTHOR . . . .

DATE READ . . . .

THE COVER

RATING   1   2   3   4   5

WHAT DREW ME TO THIS COVER/ WHAT I DIDN'T LOVE ABOUT THIS COVER

. . . .

. . . .

. . . .

WHY I CHOSE THIS BOOK . . . .

. . . .

OTHER BOOKS I HAVE READ OR PLAN TO READ BY THIS AUTHOR
(Check if read already)

○ . . . .

○ . . . .

○ . . . .

○ . . . .

THE FEELING(S) THIS BOOK EVOKED IN ME . . . .

. . . .

FAVORITE PASSAGE(S) . . . .

. . . .

. . . .

. . . .

. . . .

. . . .

. . . .

DID READING THIS BOOK CHANGE ME IN ANY WAY? . . . .

. . . .

. . . .

WHO WOULD I LIKE TO SHARE THIS BOOK WITH?
WHAT WOULD I HOPE FOR THEM TO TAKE AWAY FROM IT?

. . . .

. . . .

NOT RECOMMENDED? WHY? . . . .

REREAD?   Y   N

RATINGS

WRITING STYLE	Loved it	Just okay	Didn't enjoy
MESSAGE	Loved it	Just okay	Didn't enjoy
READING EXPERIENCE	Loved it	Just okay	Didn't enjoy

TITLE . . . .

AUTHOR . . . .

DATE READ . . . .

THE COVER

RATING   1   2   3   4   5

WHAT DREW ME TO THIS COVER/ WHAT I DIDN'T LOVE ABOUT THIS COVER

. . . .

. . . .

. . . .

WHY I CHOSE THIS BOOK . . . .

. . . .

OTHER BOOKS I HAVE READ OR PLAN TO READ BY THIS AUTHOR
(Check if read already)

◯ . . . .

◯ . . . .

◯ . . . .

◯ . . . .

THE FEELING(S) THIS BOOK EVOKED IN ME . . . .

. . . .

FAVORITE PASSAGE(S) . . . .

. . . .

. . . .

. . . .

. . . .

. . . .

. . . .

DID READING THIS BOOK CHANGE ME IN ANY WAY? . . . .

. . . .

. . . .

WHO WOULD I LIKE TO SHARE THIS BOOK WITH?
WHAT WOULD I HOPE FOR THEM TO TAKE AWAY FROM IT?

. . . .

. . . .

NOT RECOMMENDED? WHY? . . . .

REREAD?   Y   N

RATINGS

WRITING STYLE	Loved it	Just okay	Didn't enjoy
MESSAGE	Loved it	Just okay	Didn't enjoy
READING EXPERIENCE	Loved it	Just okay	Didn't enjoy

TITLE . . . .

AUTHOR . . . .

DATE READ . . . .

THE COVER

RATING   1   2   3   4   5

WHAT DREW ME TO THIS COVER/ WHAT I DIDN'T LOVE ABOUT THIS COVER

. . . .

. . . .

. . . .

WHY I CHOSE THIS BOOK . . . .

. . . .

OTHER BOOKS I HAVE READ OR PLAN TO READ BY THIS AUTHOR
(Check if read already)

◯ . . . .

◯ . . . .

◯ . . . .

◯ . . . .

THE FEELING(S) THIS BOOK EVOKED IN ME . . . .

. . . .

FAVORITE PASSAGE(S) . . . .

. . . .

. . . .

. . . .

. . . .

. . . .

. . . .

DID READING THIS BOOK CHANGE ME IN ANY WAY? . . . .

. . . .

. . . .

WHO WOULD I LIKE TO SHARE THIS BOOK WITH?
WHAT WOULD I HOPE FOR THEM TO TAKE AWAY FROM IT?

. . . .

. . . .

NOT RECOMMENDED? WHY? . . . .

REREAD?   Y   N

RATINGS

WRITING STYLE	Loved it	Just okay	Didn't enjoy
MESSAGE	Loved it	Just okay	Didn't enjoy
READING EXPERIENCE	Loved it	Just okay	Didn't enjoy

Genre Hound: Science Fiction

Science fiction is an essential genre that explores the impact of scientific concepts on humanity. It looks into the future, illuminates new worlds, postulates where humankind might go next, and explores the ideas that underpin human life and society. My favorite sci-fi:

_____

_____

_____

_____

_____

_____

_____

_____

_____

_____

_____

_____

_____

_____

_____

_____

_____

_____

TITLE . . . .

AUTHOR . . . .

DATE READ . . . .

THE COVER

RATING   1   2   3   4   5

WHAT DREW ME TO THIS COVER/ WHAT I DIDN'T LOVE ABOUT THIS COVER

. . . .

. . . .

. . . .

WHY I CHOSE THIS BOOK . . . .

. . . .

OTHER BOOKS I HAVE READ OR PLAN TO READ BY THIS AUTHOR
(Check if read already)

○ . . . .

○ . . . .

○ . . . .

○ . . . .

THE FEELING(S) THIS BOOK EVOKED IN ME . . . .

. . . .

FAVORITE PASSAGE(S) . . . .
. . . .
. . . .
. . . .
. . . .
. . . .
. . . .

DID READING THIS BOOK CHANGE ME IN ANY WAY? . . . .
. . . .
. . . .

WHO WOULD I LIKE TO SHARE THIS BOOK WITH?
WHAT WOULD I HOPE FOR THEM TO TAKE AWAY FROM IT?

. . . .
. . . .

NOT RECOMMENDED? WHY? . . . .

REREAD?   Y   N

RATINGS

WRITING STYLE	Loved it	Just okay	Didn't enjoy
MESSAGE	Loved it	Just okay	Didn't enjoy
READING EXPERIENCE	Loved it	Just okay	Didn't enjoy

TITLE . . . .

AUTHOR . . . .

DATE READ . . . .

THE COVER

RATING   1   2   3   4   5

WHAT DREW ME TO THIS COVER/ WHAT I DIDN'T LOVE ABOUT THIS COVER

. . . .

. . . .

. . . .

WHY I CHOSE THIS BOOK . . . .

. . . .

OTHER BOOKS I HAVE READ OR PLAN TO READ BY THIS AUTHOR
(Check if read already)

○ . . . .

○ . . . .

○ . . . .

○ . . . .

THE FEELING(S) THIS BOOK EVOKED IN ME . . . .

. . . .

FAVORITE PASSAGE(S) . . . .

. . . .

. . . .

. . . .

. . . .

. . . .

. . . .

DID READING THIS BOOK CHANGE ME IN ANY WAY? . . . .

. . . .

. . . .

WHO WOULD I LIKE TO SHARE THIS BOOK WITH?
WHAT WOULD I HOPE FOR THEM TO TAKE AWAY FROM IT?

. . . .

. . . .

NOT RECOMMENDED? WHY? . . . .

REREAD?   Y   N

RATINGS

WRITING STYLE	Loved it	Just okay	Didn't enjoy
MESSAGE	Loved it	Just okay	Didn't enjoy
READING EXPERIENCE	Loved it	Just okay	Didn't enjoy

TITLE . . . .

AUTHOR . . . .

DATE READ . . . .

THE COVER

RATING   1   2   3   4   5

WHAT DREW ME TO THIS COVER/ WHAT I DIDN'T LOVE ABOUT THIS COVER

. . . .

. . . .

. . . .

WHY I CHOSE THIS BOOK . . . .

. . . .

OTHER BOOKS I HAVE READ OR PLAN TO READ BY THIS AUTHOR
(Check if read already)

◯ . . . .

◯ . . . .

◯ . . . .

◯ . . . .

THE FEELING(S) THIS BOOK EVOKED IN ME . . . .

. . . .

FAVORITE PASSAGE(S) . . . .

. . . .

. . . .

. . . .

. . . .

. . . .

. . . .

DID READING THIS BOOK CHANGE ME IN ANY WAY? . . . .

. . . .

. . . .

WHO WOULD I LIKE TO SHARE THIS BOOK WITH?
WHAT WOULD I HOPE FOR THEM TO TAKE AWAY FROM IT?

. . . .

. . . .

NOT RECOMMENDED? WHY? . . . .

REREAD?   Y   N

RATINGS

WRITING STYLE	Loved it	Just okay	Didn't enjoy
MESSAGE	Loved it	Just okay	Didn't enjoy
READING EXPERIENCE	Loved it	Just okay	Didn't enjoy

TITLE . . . .

AUTHOR . . . .

DATE READ . . . .

THE COVER

RATING   1   2   3   4   5

WHAT DREW ME TO THIS COVER/ WHAT I DIDN'T LOVE ABOUT THIS COVER

. . . .

. . . .

. . . .

WHY I CHOSE THIS BOOK . . . .

. . . .

OTHER BOOKS I HAVE READ OR PLAN TO READ BY THIS AUTHOR
(Check if read already)

○ . . . .

○ . . . .

○ . . . .

○ . . . .

THE FEELING(S) THIS BOOK EVOKED IN ME . . . .

. . . .

FAVORITE PASSAGE(S) . . . .

. . . .

. . . .

. . . .

. . . .

. . . .

. . . .

DID READING THIS BOOK CHANGE ME IN ANY WAY? . . . .

. . . .

. . . .

WHO WOULD I LIKE TO SHARE THIS BOOK WITH?
WHAT WOULD I HOPE FOR THEM TO TAKE AWAY FROM IT?

. . . .

. . . .

NOT RECOMMENDED? WHY? . . . .

REREAD?   Y   N

RATINGS

WRITING STYLE	Loved it	Just okay	Didn't enjoy
MESSAGE	Loved it	Just okay	Didn't enjoy
READING EXPERIENCE	Loved it	Just okay	Didn't enjoy

Books That Changed My Life

"I read a book one day and my whole life was changed."

—Orhan Pamuk, *The New Life*

TITLE _____

HOW IT CHANGED MY LIFE _____

_____

_____

TITLE _____

HOW IT CHANGED MY LIFE _____

_____

_____

TITLE _____

HOW IT CHANGED MY LIFE _____

_____

_____

TITLE _____

HOW IT CHANGED MY LIFE _____

_____

_____

TITLE _____

HOW IT CHANGED MY LIFE _____

_____

_____

TITLE _____

HOW IT CHANGED MY LIFE _____

_____

_____

TITLE _____

HOW IT CHANGED MY LIFE _____

_____

_____

TITLE _____

HOW IT CHANGED MY LIFE _____

_____

_____

TITLE. . . . .

AUTHOR. . . . .

DATE READ. . . . .

THE COVER

RATING   1   2   3   4   5

WHAT DREW ME TO THIS COVER/ WHAT I DIDN'T LOVE ABOUT THIS COVER

. . . .

. . . .

. . . .

WHY I CHOSE THIS BOOK . . . .

. . . .

OTHER BOOKS I HAVE READ OR PLAN TO READ BY THIS AUTHOR
(Check if read already)

○ . . . .

○ . . . .

○ . . . .

○ . . . .

THE FEELING(S) THIS BOOK EVOKED IN ME . . . .

. . . .

FAVORITE PASSAGE(S) . . . .

. . . .

. . . .

. . . .

. . . .

. . . .

. . . .

DID READING THIS BOOK CHANGE ME IN ANY WAY? . . . .

. . . .

. . . .

WHO WOULD I LIKE TO SHARE THIS BOOK WITH?
WHAT WOULD I HOPE FOR THEM TO TAKE AWAY FROM IT?

. . . .

. . . .

NOT RECOMMENDED? WHY? . . . .

REREAD?   Y   N

RATINGS

WRITING STYLE	Loved it	Just okay	Didn't enjoy
MESSAGE	Loved it	Just okay	Didn't enjoy
READING EXPERIENCE	Loved it	Just okay	Didn't enjoy

TITLE . . . .

AUTHOR . . . .

DATE READ . . . .

THE COVER

RATING   1   2   3   4   5

WHAT DREW ME TO THIS COVER/ WHAT I DIDN'T LOVE ABOUT THIS COVER

. . . .

. . . .

. . . .

WHY I CHOSE THIS BOOK . . . .

. . . .

OTHER BOOKS I HAVE READ OR PLAN TO READ BY THIS AUTHOR
(Check if read already)

◯ . . . .

◯ . . . .

◯ . . . .

◯ . . . .

THE FEELING(S) THIS BOOK EVOKED IN ME . . . .

. . . .

FAVORITE PASSAGE(S) . . . .

. . . .

. . . .

. . . .

. . . .

. . . .

. . . .

DID READING THIS BOOK CHANGE ME IN ANY WAY? . . . .

. . . .

. . . .

WHO WOULD I LIKE TO SHARE THIS BOOK WITH?
WHAT WOULD I HOPE FOR THEM TO TAKE AWAY FROM IT?

. . . .

. . . .

NOT RECOMMENDED? WHY? . . . .

REREAD?   Y   N

RATINGS

WRITING STYLE	Loved it	Just okay	Didn't enjoy
MESSAGE	Loved it	Just okay	Didn't enjoy
READING EXPERIENCE	Loved it	Just okay	Didn't enjoy

TITLE . . . .

AUTHOR . . . .

DATE READ . . . .

THE COVER

RATING   1   2   3   4   5

WHAT DREW ME TO THIS COVER/ WHAT I DIDN'T LOVE ABOUT THIS COVER

. . . .

. . . .

. . . .

WHY I CHOSE THIS BOOK . . . .

. . . .

OTHER BOOKS I HAVE READ OR PLAN TO READ BY THIS AUTHOR
(Check if read already)

◯ . . . .

◯ . . . .

◯ . . . .

◯ . . . .

THE FEELING(S) THIS BOOK EVOKED IN ME . . . .

. . . .

FAVORITE PASSAGE(S) . . . .

. . . .

. . . .

. . . .

. . . .

. . . .

. . . .

DID READING THIS BOOK CHANGE ME IN ANY WAY? . . . .

. . . .

. . . .

WHO WOULD I LIKE TO SHARE THIS BOOK WITH?
WHAT WOULD I HOPE FOR THEM TO TAKE AWAY FROM IT?

. . . .

. . . .

NOT RECOMMENDED? WHY? . . . .

REREAD?   Y   N

RATINGS

WRITING STYLE	Loved it	Just okay	Didn't enjoy
MESSAGE	Loved it	Just okay	Didn't enjoy
READING EXPERIENCE	Loved it	Just okay	Didn't enjoy

TITLE . . . .

AUTHOR . . . .

DATE READ . . . .

THE COVER

RATING   1   2   3   4   5

WHAT DREW ME TO THIS COVER/ WHAT I DIDN'T LOVE ABOUT THIS COVER

. . . .

. . . .

. . . .

WHY I CHOSE THIS BOOK . . . .

. . . .

OTHER BOOKS I HAVE READ OR PLAN TO READ BY THIS AUTHOR
(Check if read already)

◯ . . . .

◯ . . . .

◯ . . . .

◯ . . . .

THE FEELING(S) THIS BOOK EVOKED IN ME . . . .

. . . .

FAVORITE PASSAGE(S) . . . .

. . . .

. . . .

. . . .

. . . .

. . . .

. . . .

DID READING THIS BOOK CHANGE ME IN ANY WAY? . . . .

. . . .

. . . .

WHO WOULD I LIKE TO SHARE THIS BOOK WITH?
WHAT WOULD I HOPE FOR THEM TO TAKE AWAY FROM IT?

. . . .

. . . .

NOT RECOMMENDED? WHY? . . . .

REREAD?   Y   N

RATINGS

WRITING STYLE	Loved it	Just okay	Didn't enjoy
MESSAGE	Loved it	Just okay	Didn't enjoy
READING EXPERIENCE	Loved it	Just okay	Didn't enjoy

Genre Hound: Romance

A good love story is emotionally satisfying, full of optimism, and offers an enjoyable escape from the banalities of everyday life while reminding us of the universal joy to be found in a genuine connection. My favorite romances:

TITLE . . . .

AUTHOR . . . .

DATE READ . . . .

THE COVER

RATING   1   2   3   4   5

WHAT DREW ME TO THIS COVER/ WHAT I DIDN'T LOVE ABOUT THIS COVER

. . . .

. . . .

. . . .

WHY I CHOSE THIS BOOK . . . .

. . . .

OTHER BOOKS I HAVE READ OR PLAN TO READ BY THIS AUTHOR
(Check if read already)

◯ . . . .

◯ . . . .

◯ . . . .

◯ . . . .

THE FEELING(S) THIS BOOK EVOKED IN ME . . . .

. . . .

FAVORITE PASSAGE(S) . . . .

. . . .

. . . .

. . . .

. . . .

. . . .

. . . .

DID READING THIS BOOK CHANGE ME IN ANY WAY? . . . .

. . . .

. . . .

WHO WOULD I LIKE TO SHARE THIS BOOK WITH?
WHAT WOULD I HOPE FOR THEM TO TAKE AWAY FROM IT?

. . . .

. . . .

NOT RECOMMENDED? WHY? . . . .

REREAD?   Y   N

RATINGS

WRITING STYLE	Loved it	Just okay	Didn't enjoy
MESSAGE	Loved it	Just okay	Didn't enjoy
READING EXPERIENCE	Loved it	Just okay	Didn't enjoy

TITLE . . . .

AUTHOR . . . .

DATE READ . . . .

THE COVER

RATING   1   2   3   4   5

WHAT DREW ME TO THIS COVER/ WHAT I DIDN'T LOVE ABOUT THIS COVER

. . . .

. . . .

. . . .

WHY I CHOSE THIS BOOK . . . .

. . . .

OTHER BOOKS I HAVE READ OR PLAN TO READ BY THIS AUTHOR
(Check if read already)

◯ . . . .

◯ . . . .

◯ . . . .

◯ . . . .

THE FEELING(S) THIS BOOK EVOKED IN ME . . . .

. . . .

FAVORITE PASSAGE(S) . . . .

. . . .

. . . .

. . . .

. . . .

. . . .

. . . .

DID READING THIS BOOK CHANGE ME IN ANY WAY? . . . .

. . . .

. . . .

WHO WOULD I LIKE TO SHARE THIS BOOK WITH?
WHAT WOULD I HOPE FOR THEM TO TAKE AWAY FROM IT?

. . . .

. . . .

NOT RECOMMENDED? WHY? . . . .

REREAD?　　　Y　　　N

RATINGS

WRITING STYLE	Loved it	Just okay	Didn't enjoy
MESSAGE	Loved it	Just okay	Didn't enjoy
READING EXPERIENCE	Loved it	Just okay	Didn't enjoy

TITLE . . . .

AUTHOR . . . .

DATE READ . . . .

THE COVER

RATING   1   2   3   4   5

WHAT DREW ME TO THIS COVER/ WHAT I DIDN'T LOVE ABOUT THIS COVER

. . . .

. . . .

. . . .

WHY I CHOSE THIS BOOK . . . .

. . . .

OTHER BOOKS I HAVE READ OR PLAN TO READ BY THIS AUTHOR
(Check if read already)

◯ . . . .

◯ . . . .

◯ . . . .

◯ . . . .

THE FEELING(S) THIS BOOK EVOKED IN ME . . . .

. . . .

FAVORITE PASSAGE(S) . . . .

. . . .

. . . .

. . . .

. . . .

. . . .

. . . .

DID READING THIS BOOK CHANGE ME IN ANY WAY? . . . .

. . . .

. . . .

WHO WOULD I LIKE TO SHARE THIS BOOK WITH?
WHAT WOULD I HOPE FOR THEM TO TAKE AWAY FROM IT?

. . . .

. . . .

NOT RECOMMENDED? WHY? . . . .

REREAD?   Y   N

RATINGS

WRITING STYLE	Loved it	Just okay	Didn't enjoy
MESSAGE	Loved it	Just okay	Didn't enjoy
READING EXPERIENCE	Loved it	Just okay	Didn't enjoy

TITLE . . . .

AUTHOR . . . .

DATE READ . . . .

THE COVER

RATING   1   2   3   4   5

WHAT DREW ME TO THIS COVER/ WHAT I DIDN'T LOVE ABOUT THIS COVER

. . . .

. . . .

. . . .

WHY I CHOSE THIS BOOK . . . .

. . . .

OTHER BOOKS I HAVE READ OR PLAN TO READ BY THIS AUTHOR
(Check if read already)

◯ . . . .

◯ . . . .

◯ . . . .

◯ . . . .

THE FEELING(S) THIS BOOK EVOKED IN ME . . . .

. . . .

FAVORITE PASSAGE(S) . . . .

. . . .

. . . .

. . . .

. . . .

. . . .

. . . .

DID READING THIS BOOK CHANGE ME IN ANY WAY? . . . .

. . . .

. . . .

WHO WOULD I LIKE TO SHARE THIS BOOK WITH?
WHAT WOULD I HOPE FOR THEM TO TAKE AWAY FROM IT?

. . . .

. . . .

NOT RECOMMENDED? WHY? . . . .

REREAD?   Y   N

RATINGS

WRITING STYLE	Loved it	Just okay	Didn't enjoy
MESSAGE	Loved it	Just okay	Didn't enjoy
READING EXPERIENCE	Loved it	Just okay	Didn't enjoy

Books I Would Like to Read Again

"A truly great book should be read in youth, again in maturity, and once more in old age, as a fine building should be seen by morning light, at noon, and by moonlight."

—Robertson Davies, *The Enthusiasms of Roberston Davies*

TITLE _____

WHY I WOULD READ IT AGAIN _____

_____

_____

TITLE _____

WHY I WOULD READ IT AGAIN _____

_____

_____

TITLE _____

WHY I WOULD READ IT AGAIN _____

_____

_____

TITLE _____

WHY I WOULD READ IT AGAIN _____

_____

_____

TITLE _____

WHY I WOULD READ IT AGAIN _____

_____

_____

TITLE _____

WHY I WOULD READ IT AGAIN _____

_____

_____

TITLE _____

WHY I WOULD READ IT AGAIN _____

_____

_____

TITLE _____

WHY I WOULD READ IT AGAIN _____

_____

_____

TITLE _____

WHY I WOULD READ IT AGAIN _____

_____

_____

TITLE . . . .

AUTHOR . . . .

DATE READ . . . .

THE COVER

RATING   1   2   3   4   5

WHAT DREW ME TO THIS COVER/ WHAT I DIDN'T LOVE ABOUT THIS COVER

. . . .

. . . .

. . . .

WHY I CHOSE THIS BOOK . . . .

. . . .

OTHER BOOKS I HAVE READ OR PLAN TO READ BY THIS AUTHOR
(Check if read already)

○ . . . .

○ . . . .

○ . . . .

○ . . . .

THE FEELING(S) THIS BOOK EVOKED IN ME . . . .

. . . .

FAVORITE PASSAGE(S) . . . .
. . . .
. . . .
. . . .
. . . .
. . . .
. . . .

DID READING THIS BOOK CHANGE ME IN ANY WAY? . . . .
. . . .
. . . .

WHO WOULD I LIKE TO SHARE THIS BOOK WITH?
WHAT WOULD I HOPE FOR THEM TO TAKE AWAY FROM IT?

. . . .
. . . .

NOT RECOMMENDED? WHY? . . . .

REREAD?   Y   N

RATINGS

WRITING STYLE	Loved it	Just okay	Didn't enjoy
MESSAGE	Loved it	Just okay	Didn't enjoy
READING EXPERIENCE	Loved it	Just okay	Didn't enjoy

TITLE . . . .

AUTHOR . . . .

DATE READ . . . .

THE COVER

RATING   1   2   3   4   5

WHAT DREW ME TO THIS COVER/ WHAT I DIDN'T LOVE ABOUT THIS COVER

. . . .

. . . .

. . . .

WHY I CHOSE THIS BOOK . . . .

. . . .

OTHER BOOKS I HAVE READ OR PLAN TO READ BY THIS AUTHOR
(Check if read already)

○ . . . .

○ . . . .

○ . . . .

○ . . . .

THE FEELING(S) THIS BOOK EVOKED IN ME . . . .

. . . .

FAVORITE PASSAGE(S) . . . .

. . . .

. . . .

. . . .

. . . .

. . . .

. . . .

DID READING THIS BOOK CHANGE ME IN ANY WAY? . . . .

. . . .

. . . .

WHO WOULD I LIKE TO SHARE THIS BOOK WITH?
WHAT WOULD I HOPE FOR THEM TO TAKE AWAY FROM IT?

. . . .

. . . .

NOT RECOMMENDED? WHY? . . . .

REREAD?   Y   N

RATINGS

WRITING STYLE	Loved it	Just okay	Didn't enjoy
MESSAGE	Loved it	Just okay	Didn't enjoy
READING EXPERIENCE	Loved it	Just okay	Didn't enjoy

TITLE . . . .

AUTHOR . . . .

DATE READ . . . .

THE COVER

RATING   1   2   3   4   5

WHAT DREW ME TO THIS COVER/ WHAT I DIDN'T LOVE ABOUT THIS COVER

. . . .

. . . .

. . . .

WHY I CHOSE THIS BOOK . . . .

. . . .

OTHER BOOKS I HAVE READ OR PLAN TO READ BY THIS AUTHOR
(Check if read already)

◯ . . . .

◯ . . . .

◯ . . . .

◯ . . . .

THE FEELING(S) THIS BOOK EVOKED IN ME . . . .

. . . .

FAVORITE PASSAGE(S) . . . .

. . . .

. . . .

. . . .

. . . .

. . . .

. . . .

DID READING THIS BOOK CHANGE ME IN ANY WAY? . . . .

. . . .

. . . .

WHO WOULD I LIKE TO SHARE THIS BOOK WITH?
WHAT WOULD I HOPE FOR THEM TO TAKE AWAY FROM IT?

. . . .

. . . .

NOT RECOMMENDED? WHY? . . . .

REREAD?   Y   N

RATINGS

WRITING STYLE	Loved it	Just okay	Didn't enjoy
MESSAGE	Loved it	Just okay	Didn't enjoy
READING EXPERIENCE	Loved it	Just okay	Didn't enjoy

TITLE . . . .

AUTHOR . . . .

DATE READ . . . .

THE COVER

RATING   1   2   3   4   5

WHAT DREW ME TO THIS COVER/ WHAT I DIDN'T LOVE ABOUT THIS COVER

. . . .

. . . .

. . . .

WHY I CHOSE THIS BOOK . . . .

. . . .

OTHER BOOKS I HAVE READ OR PLAN TO READ BY THIS AUTHOR
(Check if read already)

◯ . . . .

◯ . . . .

◯ . . . .

◯ . . . .

THE FEELING(S) THIS BOOK EVOKED IN ME . . . .

. . . .

FAVORITE PASSAGE(S) . . . .

. . . .

. . . .

. . . .

. . . .

. . . .

. . . .

DID READING THIS BOOK CHANGE ME IN ANY WAY? . . . .

. . . .

. . . .

WHO WOULD I LIKE TO SHARE THIS BOOK WITH?
WHAT WOULD I HOPE FOR THEM TO TAKE AWAY FROM IT?

. . . .

. . . .

NOT RECOMMENDED? WHY? . . . .

REREAD?   Y   N

RATINGS

WRITING STYLE	Loved it	Just okay	Didn't enjoy
MESSAGE	Loved it	Just okay	Didn't enjoy
READING EXPERIENCE	Loved it	Just okay	Didn't enjoy

Genre Hound: Horror

Sometimes, you just want the delicious pleasure of feeling scared. A good horror story takes readers to dangerous and dark places without actually endangering anyone, allowing us to enjoy the thrills and chills vicariously. My favorite horror stories:

_____

_____

_____

_____

_____

_____

_____

_____

_____

_____

_____

_____

_____

_____

_____

_____

_____

_____

_____

TITLE . . . .

AUTHOR . . . .

DATE READ . . . .

THE COVER

RATING   1   2   3   4   5

WHAT DREW ME TO THIS COVER/ WHAT I DIDN'T LOVE ABOUT THIS COVER

. . . .

. . . .

. . . .

WHY I CHOSE THIS BOOK . . . .

. . . .

OTHER BOOKS I HAVE READ OR PLAN TO READ BY THIS AUTHOR
(Check if read already)

◯ . . . .

◯ . . . .

◯ . . . .

◯ . . . .

THE FEELING(S) THIS BOOK EVOKED IN ME . . . .

. . . .

FAVORITE PASSAGE(S) . . . .

. . . .

. . . .

. . . .

. . . .

. . . .

. . . .

DID READING THIS BOOK CHANGE ME IN ANY WAY? . . . .

. . . .

. . . .

WHO WOULD I LIKE TO SHARE THIS BOOK WITH?
WHAT WOULD I HOPE FOR THEM TO TAKE AWAY FROM IT?

. . . .

. . . .

NOT RECOMMENDED? WHY? . . . .

REREAD?   Y   N

RATINGS

WRITING STYLE	Loved it	Just okay	Didn't enjoy
MESSAGE	Loved it	Just okay	Didn't enjoy
READING EXPERIENCE	Loved it	Just okay	Didn't enjoy

TITLE . . . .

AUTHOR . . . .

DATE READ . . . .

THE COVER

RATING   1   2   3   4   5

WHAT DREW ME TO THIS COVER/ WHAT I DIDN'T LOVE ABOUT THIS COVER

. . . .

. . . .

. . . .

WHY I CHOSE THIS BOOK . . . .

. . . .

OTHER BOOKS I HAVE READ OR PLAN TO READ BY THIS AUTHOR
(Check if read already)

○ . . . .

○ . . . .

○ . . . .

○ . . . .

THE FEELING(S) THIS BOOK EVOKED IN ME . . . .

. . . .

FAVORITE PASSAGE(S) . . . .

. . . .

. . . .

. . . .

. . . .

. . . .

. . . .

DID READING THIS BOOK CHANGE ME IN ANY WAY? . . . .

. . . .

. . . .

WHO WOULD I LIKE TO SHARE THIS BOOK WITH?
WHAT WOULD I HOPE FOR THEM TO TAKE AWAY FROM IT?

. . . .

. . . .

NOT RECOMMENDED? WHY? . . . .

REREAD?   Y   N

RATINGS

WRITING STYLE	Loved it	Just okay	Didn't enjoy
MESSAGE	Loved it	Just okay	Didn't enjoy
READING EXPERIENCE	Loved it	Just okay	Didn't enjoy

TITLE . . . .

AUTHOR . . . .

DATE READ . . . .

THE COVER

RATING   1   2   3   4   5

WHAT DREW ME TO THIS COVER/ WHAT I DIDN'T LOVE ABOUT THIS COVER

. . . .

. . . .

. . . .

WHY I CHOSE THIS BOOK . . . .

. . . .

OTHER BOOKS I HAVE READ OR PLAN TO READ BY THIS AUTHOR
(Check if read already)

    ◯ . . . .

    ◯ . . . .

    ◯ . . . .

    ◯ . . . .

THE FEELING(S) THIS BOOK EVOKED IN ME . . . .

. . . .

FAVORITE PASSAGE(S) . . . .

. . . .

. . . .

. . . .

. . . .

. . . .

. . . .

DID READING THIS BOOK CHANGE ME IN ANY WAY? . . . .

. . . .

. . . .

WHO WOULD I LIKE TO SHARE THIS BOOK WITH?
WHAT WOULD I HOPE FOR THEM TO TAKE AWAY FROM IT?

. . . .

. . . .

NOT RECOMMENDED? WHY? . . . .

REREAD?   Y   N

RATINGS

WRITING STYLE	Loved it	Just okay	Didn't enjoy
MESSAGE	Loved it	Just okay	Didn't enjoy
READING EXPERIENCE	Loved it	Just okay	Didn't enjoy

TITLE . . . .

AUTHOR . . . .

DATE READ . . . .

THE COVER

RATING   1   2   3   4   5

WHAT DREW ME TO THIS COVER/ WHAT I DIDN'T LOVE ABOUT THIS COVER

. . . .

. . . .

. . . .

WHY I CHOSE THIS BOOK . . . .

. . . .

OTHER BOOKS I HAVE READ OR PLAN TO READ BY THIS AUTHOR
(Check if read already)

◯ . . . .

◯ . . . .

◯ . . . .

◯ . . . .

THE FEELING(S) THIS BOOK EVOKED IN ME . . . .

. . . .

FAVORITE PASSAGE(S) . . . .

. . . .

. . . .

. . . .

. . . .

. . . .

. . . .

DID READING THIS BOOK CHANGE ME IN ANY WAY? . . . .

. . . .

. . . .

WHO WOULD I LIKE TO SHARE THIS BOOK WITH?
WHAT WOULD I HOPE FOR THEM TO TAKE AWAY FROM IT?

. . . .

. . . .

NOT RECOMMENDED? WHY? . . . .

REREAD?   Y   N

RATINGS

WRITING STYLE	Loved it	Just okay	Didn't enjoy
MESSAGE	Loved it	Just okay	Didn't enjoy
READING EXPERIENCE	Loved it	Just okay	Didn't enjoy

Books That I Bought for the Cover

TITLE . . . .

AUTHOR . . . .

DATE READ . . . .

THE COVER

RATING   1   2   3   4   5

WHAT DREW ME TO THIS COVER/ WHAT I DIDN'T LOVE ABOUT THIS COVER

. . . .

. . . .

. . . .

WHY I CHOSE THIS BOOK . . . .

. . . .

OTHER BOOKS I HAVE READ OR PLAN TO READ BY THIS AUTHOR
(Check if read already)

◯ . . . .

◯ . . . .

◯ . . . .

◯ . . . .

THE FEELING(S) THIS BOOK EVOKED IN ME . . . .

. . . .

FAVORITE PASSAGE(S) . . . .

. . . .

. . . .

. . . .

. . . .

. . . .

. . . .

DID READING THIS BOOK CHANGE ME IN ANY WAY? . . . .

. . . .

. . . .

WHO WOULD I LIKE TO SHARE THIS BOOK WITH?
WHAT WOULD I HOPE FOR THEM TO TAKE AWAY FROM IT?

. . . .

. . . .

NOT RECOMMENDED? WHY? . . . .

REREAD?   Y   N

RATINGS

WRITING STYLE	Loved it	Just okay	Didn't enjoy
MESSAGE	Loved it	Just okay	Didn't enjoy
READING EXPERIENCE	Loved it	Just okay	Didn't enjoy

TITLE . . . .

AUTHOR . . . .

DATE READ . . . .

THE COVER

RATING   1   2   3   4   5

WHAT DREW ME TO THIS COVER/ WHAT I DIDN'T LOVE ABOUT THIS COVER

. . . .

. . . .

. . . .

WHY I CHOSE THIS BOOK . . . .

. . . .

OTHER BOOKS I HAVE READ OR PLAN TO READ BY THIS AUTHOR
(Check if read already)

○ . . . .

○ . . . .

○ . . . .

○ . . . .

THE FEELING(S) THIS BOOK EVOKED IN ME . . . .

. . . .

FAVORITE PASSAGE(S) . . . .

. . . .

. . . .

. . . .

. . . .

. . . .

. . . .

DID READING THIS BOOK CHANGE ME IN ANY WAY? . . . .

. . . .

. . . .

WHO WOULD I LIKE TO SHARE THIS BOOK WITH?
WHAT WOULD I HOPE FOR THEM TO TAKE AWAY FROM IT?

. . . .

. . . .

NOT RECOMMENDED? WHY? . . . .

REREAD?   Y   N

RATINGS

WRITING STYLE	Loved it	Just okay	Didn't enjoy
MESSAGE	Loved it	Just okay	Didn't enjoy
READING EXPERIENCE	Loved it	Just okay	Didn't enjoy

TITLE . . . .

AUTHOR . . . .

DATE READ . . . .

THE COVER

RATING   1   2   3   4   5

WHAT DREW ME TO THIS COVER/ WHAT I DIDN'T LOVE ABOUT THIS COVER

. . . .

. . . .

. . . .

WHY I CHOSE THIS BOOK . . . .

. . . .

OTHER BOOKS I HAVE READ OR PLAN TO READ BY THIS AUTHOR
(Check if read already)

    ○ . . . .

    ○ . . . .

    ○ . . . .

    ○ . . . .

THE FEELING(S) THIS BOOK EVOKED IN ME . . . .

. . . .

FAVORITE PASSAGE(S) . . . .

. . . .

. . . .

. . . .

. . . .

. . . .

. . . .

DID READING THIS BOOK CHANGE ME IN ANY WAY? . . . .

. . . .

. . . .

WHO WOULD I LIKE TO SHARE THIS BOOK WITH?
WHAT WOULD I HOPE FOR THEM TO TAKE AWAY FROM IT?

. . . .

. . . .

NOT RECOMMENDED? WHY? . . . .

REREAD?   Y   N

RATINGS

WRITING STYLE	Loved it	Just okay	Didn't enjoy
MESSAGE	Loved it	Just okay	Didn't enjoy
READING EXPERIENCE	Loved it	Just okay	Didn't enjoy

TITLE . . . .

AUTHOR . . . .

DATE READ . . . .

THE COVER

RATING   1   2   3   4   5

WHAT DREW ME TO THIS COVER/ WHAT I DIDN'T LOVE ABOUT THIS COVER

. . . .

. . . .

. . . .

WHY I CHOSE THIS BOOK . . . .

. . . .

OTHER BOOKS I HAVE READ OR PLAN TO READ BY THIS AUTHOR
(Check if read already)

◯ . . . .

◯ . . . .

◯ . . . .

◯ . . . .

THE FEELING(S) THIS BOOK EVOKED IN ME . . . .

. . . .

FAVORITE PASSAGE(S) . . . .

. . . .

. . . .

. . . .

. . . .

. . . .

. . . .

DID READING THIS BOOK CHANGE ME IN ANY WAY? . . . .

. . . .

. . . .

WHO WOULD I LIKE TO SHARE THIS BOOK WITH?
WHAT WOULD I HOPE FOR THEM TO TAKE AWAY FROM IT?

. . . .

. . . .

NOT RECOMMENDED? WHY? . . . .

REREAD?   Y   N

RATINGS

WRITING STYLE	Loved it	Just okay	Didn't enjoy
MESSAGE	Loved it	Just okay	Didn't enjoy
READING EXPERIENCE	Loved it	Just okay	Didn't enjoy

Genre Hound: Memoir and Biography

What a privilege to be able to explore someone else's life! Books that tell the story of a life or illuminate a pivotal experience give us a glimpse of what it's like to walk in someone else's shoes. My favorite memoirs and biographies:

TITLE . . . .

AUTHOR . . . .

DATE READ . . . .

THE COVER

RATING   1   2   3   4   5

WHAT DREW ME TO THIS COVER/ WHAT I DIDN'T LOVE ABOUT THIS COVER

. . . .

. . . .

. . . .

WHY I CHOSE THIS BOOK . . . .

. . . .

OTHER BOOKS I HAVE READ OR PLAN TO READ BY THIS AUTHOR
(Check if read already)

◯ . . . .

◯ . . . .

◯ . . . .

◯ . . . .

THE FEELING(S) THIS BOOK EVOKED IN ME . . . .

. . . .

FAVORITE PASSAGE(S) . . . .

. . . .

. . . .

. . . .

. . . .

. . . .

. . . .

DID READING THIS BOOK CHANGE ME IN ANY WAY? . . . .

. . . .

. . . .

WHO WOULD I LIKE TO SHARE THIS BOOK WITH?
WHAT WOULD I HOPE FOR THEM TO TAKE AWAY FROM IT?

. . . .

. . . .

NOT RECOMMENDED? WHY? . . . .

REREAD?   Y   N

RATINGS

WRITING STYLE	Loved it	Just okay	Didn't enjoy
MESSAGE	Loved it	Just okay	Didn't enjoy
READING EXPERIENCE	Loved it	Just okay	Didn't enjoy

TITLE . . . .

AUTHOR . . . .

DATE READ . . . .

THE COVER

RATING   1   2   3   4   5

WHAT DREW ME TO THIS COVER/ WHAT I DIDN'T LOVE ABOUT THIS COVER

. . . .

. . . .

. . . .

WHY I CHOSE THIS BOOK . . . .

. . . .

OTHER BOOKS I HAVE READ OR PLAN TO READ BY THIS AUTHOR
(Check if read already)

◯ . . . .

◯ . . . .

◯ . . . .

◯ . . . .

THE FEELING(S) THIS BOOK EVOKED IN ME . . . .

. . . .

FAVORITE PASSAGE(S) . . . .

. . . .

. . . .

. . . .

. . . .

. . . .

. . . .

DID READING THIS BOOK CHANGE ME IN ANY WAY? . . . .

. . . .

. . . .

WHO WOULD I LIKE TO SHARE THIS BOOK WITH?
WHAT WOULD I HOPE FOR THEM TO TAKE AWAY FROM IT?

. . . .

. . . .

NOT RECOMMENDED? WHY? . . . .

REREAD?   Y   N

RATINGS

WRITING STYLE	Loved it	Just okay	Didn't enjoy
MESSAGE	Loved it	Just okay	Didn't enjoy
READING EXPERIENCE	Loved it	Just okay	Didn't enjoy

TITLE . . . .

AUTHOR . . . .

DATE READ . . . .

THE COVER

RATING   1   2   3   4   5

WHAT DREW ME TO THIS COVER/ WHAT I DIDN'T LOVE ABOUT THIS COVER

. . . .

. . . .

. . . .

WHY I CHOSE THIS BOOK . . . .

. . . .

OTHER BOOKS I HAVE READ OR PLAN TO READ BY THIS AUTHOR
(Check if read already)

◯ . . . .

◯ . . . .

◯ . . . .

◯ . . . .

THE FEELING(S) THIS BOOK EVOKED IN ME . . . .

. . . .

FAVORITE PASSAGE(S) . . . .

. . . .

. . . .

. . . .

. . . .

. . . .

. . . .

DID READING THIS BOOK CHANGE ME IN ANY WAY? . . . .

. . . .

. . . .

WHO WOULD I LIKE TO SHARE THIS BOOK WITH?
WHAT WOULD I HOPE FOR THEM TO TAKE AWAY FROM IT?

. . . .

. . . .

NOT RECOMMENDED? WHY? . . . .

REREAD?   Y   N

RATINGS

WRITING STYLE	Loved it	Just okay	Didn't enjoy
MESSAGE	Loved it	Just okay	Didn't enjoy
READING EXPERIENCE	Loved it	Just okay	Didn't enjoy

TITLE . . . .

AUTHOR . . . .

DATE READ . . . .

THE COVER

RATING   1   2   3   4   5

WHAT DREW ME TO THIS COVER/ WHAT I DIDN'T LOVE ABOUT THIS COVER

. . . .

. . . .

. . . .

WHY I CHOSE THIS BOOK . . . .

. . . .

OTHER BOOKS I HAVE READ OR PLAN TO READ BY THIS AUTHOR
(Check if read already)

◯ . . . .

◯ . . . .

◯ . . . .

◯ . . . .

THE FEELING(S) THIS BOOK EVOKED IN ME . . . .

. . . .

FAVORITE PASSAGE(S) . . . .

. . . .

. . . .

. . . .

. . . .

. . . .

. . . .

DID READING THIS BOOK CHANGE ME IN ANY WAY? . . . .

. . . .

. . . .

WHO WOULD I LIKE TO SHARE THIS BOOK WITH?
WHAT WOULD I HOPE FOR THEM TO TAKE AWAY FROM IT?

. . . .

. . . .

NOT RECOMMENDED? WHY? . . . .

REREAD?   Y   N

RATINGS

WRITING STYLE	Loved it	Just okay	Didn't enjoy
MESSAGE	Loved it	Just okay	Didn't enjoy
READING EXPERIENCE	Loved it	Just okay	Didn't enjoy

The Books That Made Me Who I Am

"I am not influenced by books. Instead, I am shaped by them.
I am made of flesh and bone and blood. I am also made of books."

—Roxane Gay

TITLE . . . .

AUTHOR . . . .

DATE READ . . . .

THE COVER

RATING   1   2   3   4   5

WHAT DREW ME TO THIS COVER/ WHAT I DIDN'T LOVE ABOUT THIS COVER

. . . .

. . . .

. . . .

WHY I CHOSE THIS BOOK . . . .

. . . .

OTHER BOOKS I HAVE READ OR PLAN TO READ BY THIS AUTHOR
(Check if read already)

◯ . . . .

◯ . . . .

◯ . . . .

◯ . . . .

THE FEELING(S) THIS BOOK EVOKED IN ME . . . .

. . . .

FAVORITE PASSAGE(S) . . . .

. . . .

. . . .

. . . .

. . . .

. . . .

. . . .

DID READING THIS BOOK CHANGE ME IN ANY WAY? . . . .

. . . .

. . . .

WHO WOULD I LIKE TO SHARE THIS BOOK WITH?
WHAT WOULD I HOPE FOR THEM TO TAKE AWAY FROM IT?

. . . .

. . . .

NOT RECOMMENDED? WHY? . . . .

REREAD?   Y   N

RATINGS

WRITING STYLE	Loved it	Just okay	Didn't enjoy
MESSAGE	Loved it	Just okay	Didn't enjoy
READING EXPERIENCE	Loved it	Just okay	Didn't enjoy

TITLE . . . .

AUTHOR . . . .

DATE READ . . . .

THE COVER

RATING   1   2   3   4   5

WHAT DREW ME TO THIS COVER/ WHAT I DIDN'T LOVE ABOUT THIS COVER

. . . .

. . . .

. . . .

WHY I CHOSE THIS BOOK . . . .

. . . .

OTHER BOOKS I HAVE READ OR PLAN TO READ BY THIS AUTHOR
(Check if read already)

◯ . . . .

◯ . . . .

◯ . . . .

◯ . . . .

THE FEELING(S) THIS BOOK EVOKED IN ME . . . .

. . . .

FAVORITE PASSAGE(S) . . . .

. . . .

. . . .

. . . .

. . . .

. . . .

. . . .

DID READING THIS BOOK CHANGE ME IN ANY WAY? . . . .

. . . .

. . . .

WHO WOULD I LIKE TO SHARE THIS BOOK WITH?
WHAT WOULD I HOPE FOR THEM TO TAKE AWAY FROM IT?

. . . .

. . . .

NOT RECOMMENDED? WHY? . . . .

REREAD?   Y   N

RATINGS

WRITING STYLE	Loved it	Just okay	Didn't enjoy
MESSAGE	Loved it	Just okay	Didn't enjoy
READING EXPERIENCE	Loved it	Just okay	Didn't enjoy

TITLE . . . .

AUTHOR . . . .

DATE READ . . . .

THE COVER

RATING   1   2   3   4   5

WHAT DREW ME TO THIS COVER/ WHAT I DIDN'T LOVE ABOUT THIS COVER

. . . .

. . . .

. . . .

WHY I CHOSE THIS BOOK . . . .

. . . .

OTHER BOOKS I HAVE READ OR PLAN TO READ BY THIS AUTHOR
(Check if read already)

◯ . . . .

◯ . . . .

◯ . . . .

◯ . . . .

THE FEELING(S) THIS BOOK EVOKED IN ME . . . .

. . . .

FAVORITE PASSAGE(S) . . . .

. . . .

. . . .

. . . .

. . . .

. . . .

. . . .

DID READING THIS BOOK CHANGE ME IN ANY WAY? . . . .

. . . .

. . . .

WHO WOULD I LIKE TO SHARE THIS BOOK WITH?
WHAT WOULD I HOPE FOR THEM TO TAKE AWAY FROM IT?

. . . .

. . . .

NOT RECOMMENDED? WHY? . . . .

REREAD?   Y   N

RATINGS

WRITING STYLE	Loved it	Just okay	Didn't enjoy
MESSAGE	Loved it	Just okay	Didn't enjoy
READING EXPERIENCE	Loved it	Just okay	Didn't enjoy

TITLE . . . .

AUTHOR . . . .

DATE READ . . . .

THE COVER

RATING   1   2   3   4   5

WHAT DREW ME TO THIS COVER/ WHAT I DIDN'T LOVE ABOUT THIS COVER

. . . .

. . . .

. . . .

WHY I CHOSE THIS BOOK . . . .

. . . .

OTHER BOOKS I HAVE READ OR PLAN TO READ BY THIS AUTHOR
(Check if read already)

◯ . . . .

◯ . . . .

◯ . . . .

◯ . . . .

THE FEELING(S) THIS BOOK EVOKED IN ME . . . .

. . . .

FAVORITE PASSAGE(S) . . . .

. . . .

. . . .

. . . .

. . . .

. . . .

. . . .

DID READING THIS BOOK CHANGE ME IN ANY WAY? . . . .

. . . .

. . . .

WHO WOULD I LIKE TO SHARE THIS BOOK WITH?
WHAT WOULD I HOPE FOR THEM TO TAKE AWAY FROM IT?

. . . .

. . . .

NOT RECOMMENDED? WHY? . . . .

REREAD?   Y   N

RATINGS

WRITING STYLE	Loved it	Just okay	Didn't enjoy
MESSAGE	Loved it	Just okay	Didn't enjoy
READING EXPERIENCE	Loved it	Just okay	Didn't enjoy

Genre Hound: Cooking

How delightful to open a new or favorite cookbook, anticipating the pleasure to be had from the recipes inside. My favorite cookbooks:

_____

_____

_____

_____

_____

_____

_____

_____

_____

_____

_____

_____

_____

_____

_____

_____

_____

_____

_____

TITLE . . . .

AUTHOR . . . .

DATE READ . . . .

THE COVER

RATING   1   2   3   4   5

WHAT DREW ME TO THIS COVER/ WHAT I DIDN'T LOVE ABOUT THIS COVER

. . . .

. . . .

. . . .

WHY I CHOSE THIS BOOK . . . .

. . . .

OTHER BOOKS I HAVE READ OR PLAN TO READ BY THIS AUTHOR
(Check if read already)

   ◯ . . . .

   ◯ . . . .

   ◯ . . . .

   ◯ . . . .

THE FEELING(S) THIS BOOK EVOKED IN ME . . . .

. . . .

FAVORITE PASSAGE(S) . . . .

. . . .

. . . .

. . . .

. . . .

. . . .

. . . .

DID READING THIS BOOK CHANGE ME IN ANY WAY? . . . .

. . . .

. . . .

WHO WOULD I LIKE TO SHARE THIS BOOK WITH?
WHAT WOULD I HOPE FOR THEM TO TAKE AWAY FROM IT?

. . . .

. . . .

NOT RECOMMENDED? WHY? . . . .

REREAD?   Y   N

RATINGS

WRITING STYLE	Loved it	Just okay	Didn't enjoy
MESSAGE	Loved it	Just okay	Didn't enjoy
READING EXPERIENCE	Loved it	Just okay	Didn't enjoy

TITLE . . . .

AUTHOR . . . .

DATE READ . . . .

THE COVER

RATING   1   2   3   4   5

WHAT DREW ME TO THIS COVER/ WHAT I DIDN'T LOVE ABOUT THIS COVER

. . . .

. . . .

. . . .

WHY I CHOSE THIS BOOK . . . .

. . . .

OTHER BOOKS I HAVE READ OR PLAN TO READ BY THIS AUTHOR
(Check if read already)

◯ . . . .

◯ . . . .

◯ . . . .

◯ . . . .

THE FEELING(S) THIS BOOK EVOKED IN ME . . . .

. . . .

FAVORITE PASSAGE(S) . . . .

. . . .

. . . .

. . . .

. . . .

. . . .

. . . .

DID READING THIS BOOK CHANGE ME IN ANY WAY? . . . .

. . . .

. . . .

WHO WOULD I LIKE TO SHARE THIS BOOK WITH?
WHAT WOULD I HOPE FOR THEM TO TAKE AWAY FROM IT?

. . . .

. . . .

NOT RECOMMENDED? WHY? . . . .

REREAD?   Y   N

RATINGS

WRITING STYLE	Loved it	Just okay	Didn't enjoy
MESSAGE	Loved it	Just okay	Didn't enjoy
READING EXPERIENCE	Loved it	Just okay	Didn't enjoy

TITLE . . . .

AUTHOR . . . .

DATE READ . . . .

THE COVER

RATING   1   2   3   4   5

WHAT DREW ME TO THIS COVER/ WHAT I DIDN'T LOVE ABOUT THIS COVER

. . . .

. . . .

. . . .

WHY I CHOSE THIS BOOK . . . .

. . . .

OTHER BOOKS I HAVE READ OR PLAN TO READ BY THIS AUTHOR
(Check if read already)

◯ . . . .

◯ . . . .

◯ . . . .

◯ . . . .

THE FEELING(S) THIS BOOK EVOKED IN ME . . . .

. . . .

FAVORITE PASSAGE(S) . . . .

. . . .

. . . .

. . . .

. . . .

. . . .

. . . .

DID READING THIS BOOK CHANGE ME IN ANY WAY? . . . .

. . . .

. . . .

WHO WOULD I LIKE TO SHARE THIS BOOK WITH?
WHAT WOULD I HOPE FOR THEM TO TAKE AWAY FROM IT?

. . . .

. . . .

NOT RECOMMENDED? WHY? . . . .

REREAD?   Y   N

RATINGS

WRITING STYLE	Loved it	Just okay	Didn't enjoy
MESSAGE	Loved it	Just okay	Didn't enjoy
READING EXPERIENCE	Loved it	Just okay	Didn't enjoy

TITLE . . . .

AUTHOR . . . .

DATE READ . . . .

THE COVER

RATING   1   2   3   4   5

WHAT DREW ME TO THIS COVER/ WHAT I DIDN'T LOVE ABOUT THIS COVER

. . . .

. . . .

. . . .

WHY I CHOSE THIS BOOK . . . .

. . . .

OTHER BOOKS I HAVE READ OR PLAN TO READ BY THIS AUTHOR
(Check if read already)

◯ . . . .

◯ . . . .

◯ . . . .

◯ . . . .

THE FEELING(S) THIS BOOK EVOKED IN ME . . . .

. . . .

FAVORITE PASSAGE(S) . . . .

. . . .

. . . .

. . . .

. . . .

. . . .

. . . .

DID READING THIS BOOK CHANGE ME IN ANY WAY? . . . .

. . . .

. . . .

WHO WOULD I LIKE TO SHARE THIS BOOK WITH?
WHAT WOULD I HOPE FOR THEM TO TAKE AWAY FROM IT?

. . . .

. . . .

NOT RECOMMENDED? WHY? . . . .

REREAD?   Y   N

RATINGS

WRITING STYLE	Loved it	Just okay	Didn't enjoy
MESSAGE	Loved it	Just okay	Didn't enjoy
READING EXPERIENCE	Loved it	Just okay	Didn't enjoy

Genre Hound: Graphic Novel

The great pleasure of a graphic novel is the marriage of images and text in service of a story, fiction or nonfiction, that an author wants to show as well as tell you. My favorite graphic novels:

_____

_____

_____

_____

_____

_____

_____

_____

_____

_____

_____

_____

_____

_____

_____

_____

_____

TITLE . . . .

AUTHOR . . . .

DATE READ . . . .

THE COVER

RATING   1   2   3   4   5

WHAT DREW ME TO THIS COVER/ WHAT I DIDN'T LOVE ABOUT THIS COVER

. . . .

. . . .

. . . .

WHY I CHOSE THIS BOOK . . . .

. . . .

OTHER BOOKS I HAVE READ OR PLAN TO READ BY THIS AUTHOR
(Check if read already)

○ . . . .

○ . . . .

○ . . . .

○ . . . .

THE FEELING(S) THIS BOOK EVOKED IN ME . . . .

. . . .

FAVORITE PASSAGE(S) . . . .

. . . .

. . . .

. . . .

. . . .

. . . .

. . . .

DID READING THIS BOOK CHANGE ME IN ANY WAY? . . . .

. . . .

. . . .

WHO WOULD I LIKE TO SHARE THIS BOOK WITH?
WHAT WOULD I HOPE FOR THEM TO TAKE AWAY FROM IT?

. . . .

. . . .

NOT RECOMMENDED? WHY? . . . .

REREAD?   Y   N

RATINGS

WRITING STYLE	Loved it	Just okay	Didn't enjoy
MESSAGE	Loved it	Just okay	Didn't enjoy
READING EXPERIENCE	Loved it	Just okay	Didn't enjoy

TITLE . . . .

AUTHOR . . . .

DATE READ . . . .

THE COVER

RATING   1   2   3   4   5

WHAT DREW ME TO THIS COVER/ WHAT I DIDN'T LOVE ABOUT THIS COVER

. . . .

. . . .

. . . .

WHY I CHOSE THIS BOOK . . . .

. . . .

OTHER BOOKS I HAVE READ OR PLAN TO READ BY THIS AUTHOR
(Check if read already)

◯ . . . .

◯ . . . .

◯ . . . .

◯ . . . .

THE FEELING(S) THIS BOOK EVOKED IN ME . . . .

. . . .

FAVORITE PASSAGE(S) . . . .

. . . .

. . . .

. . . .

. . . .

. . . .

. . . .

DID READING THIS BOOK CHANGE ME IN ANY WAY? . . . .

. . . .

. . . .

WHO WOULD I LIKE TO SHARE THIS BOOK WITH?
WHAT WOULD I HOPE FOR THEM TO TAKE AWAY FROM IT?

. . . .

. . . .

NOT RECOMMENDED? WHY? . . . .

REREAD?   Y   N

RATINGS

WRITING STYLE	Loved it	Just okay	Didn't enjoy
MESSAGE	Loved it	Just okay	Didn't enjoy
READING EXPERIENCE	Loved it	Just okay	Didn't enjoy

TITLE. . . . .

AUTHOR . . . .

DATE READ . . . .

THE COVER

RATING   1   2   3   4   5

WHAT DREW ME TO THIS COVER/ WHAT I DIDN'T LOVE ABOUT THIS COVER

. . . .

. . . .

. . . .

WHY I CHOSE THIS BOOK . . . .

. . . .

OTHER BOOKS I HAVE READ OR PLAN TO READ BY THIS AUTHOR
(Check if read already)

◯ . . . .

◯ . . . .

◯ . . . .

◯ . . . .

THE FEELING(S) THIS BOOK EVOKED IN ME . . . .

. . . .

FAVORITE PASSAGE(S) . . . .

. . . .

. . . .

. . . .

. . . .

. . . .

. . . .

DID READING THIS BOOK CHANGE ME IN ANY WAY? . . . .

. . . .

. . . .

WHO WOULD I LIKE TO SHARE THIS BOOK WITH?
WHAT WOULD I HOPE FOR THEM TO TAKE AWAY FROM IT?

. . . .

. . . .

NOT RECOMMENDED? WHY? . . . .

REREAD?   Y   N

RATINGS

WRITING STYLE	Loved it	Just okay	Didn't enjoy
MESSAGE	Loved it	Just okay	Didn't enjoy
READING EXPERIENCE	Loved it	Just okay	Didn't enjoy

TITLE . . . .

AUTHOR . . . .

DATE READ . . . .

THE COVER

RATING   1   2   3   4   5

WHAT DREW ME TO THIS COVER/ WHAT I DIDN'T LOVE ABOUT THIS COVER

. . . .

. . . .

. . . .

WHY I CHOSE THIS BOOK . . . .

. . . .

OTHER BOOKS I HAVE READ OR PLAN TO READ BY THIS AUTHOR
(Check if read already)

◯ . . . .

◯ . . . .

◯ . . . .

◯ . . . .

THE FEELING(S) THIS BOOK EVOKED IN ME . . . .

. . . .

FAVORITE PASSAGE(S) . . . .

. . . .

. . . .

. . . .

. . . .

. . . .

. . . .

DID READING THIS BOOK CHANGE ME IN ANY WAY? . . . .

. . . .

. . . .

WHO WOULD I LIKE TO SHARE THIS BOOK WITH?
WHAT WOULD I HOPE FOR THEM TO TAKE AWAY FROM IT?

. . . .

. . . .

NOT RECOMMENDED? WHY? . . . .

REREAD?   Y   N

RATINGS

WRITING STYLE	Loved it	Just okay	Didn't enjoy
MESSAGE	Loved it	Just okay	Didn't enjoy
READING EXPERIENCE	Loved it	Just okay	Didn't enjoy

Favorite and Memorable Bookstores

"So often, in the past as well, a visit to a bookshop has cheered me up and reminded me that there are good things in the world."

—Vincent van Gogh, in a Letter to Theo van Gogh, October 30, 1877

BOOKSTORE _____

LOCATION _____

WHY VISIT _____

_____

BOOKSTORE _____

LOCATION _____

WHY VISIT _____

_____

BOOKSTORE _____

LOCATION _____

WHY VISIT _____

_____

BOOKSTORE _____

LOCATION _____

WHY VISIT _____

_____

BOOKSTORE _____

LOCATION _____

WHY VISIT _____

_____

BOOKSTORE _____

LOCATION _____

WHY VISIT _____

_____

BOOKSTORE _____

LOCATION _____

WHY VISIT _____

_____

BOOKSTORE _____

LOCATION _____

WHY VISIT _____

_____

BOOKSTORE _____

LOCATION _____

WHY VISIT _____

_____

TITLE . . . .

AUTHOR . . . .

DATE READ . . . .

THE COVER

RATING   1   2   3   4   5

WHAT DREW ME TO THIS COVER/ WHAT I DIDN'T LOVE ABOUT THIS COVER

. . . .

. . . .

. . . .

WHY I CHOSE THIS BOOK . . . .

. . . .

OTHER BOOKS I HAVE READ OR PLAN TO READ BY THIS AUTHOR
(Check if read already)

○ . . . .

○ . . . .

○ . . . .

○ . . . .

THE FEELING(S) THIS BOOK EVOKED IN ME . . . .

. . . .

FAVORITE PASSAGE(S) . . . .

. . . .

. . . .

. . . .

. . . .

. . . .

. . . .

DID READING THIS BOOK CHANGE ME IN ANY WAY? . . . .

. . . .

. . . .

WHO WOULD I LIKE TO SHARE THIS BOOK WITH?
WHAT WOULD I HOPE FOR THEM TO TAKE AWAY FROM IT?

. . . .

. . . .

NOT RECOMMENDED? WHY? . . . .

REREAD?   Y   N

RATINGS

WRITING STYLE	Loved it	Just okay	Didn't enjoy
MESSAGE	Loved it	Just okay	Didn't enjoy
READING EXPERIENCE	Loved it	Just okay	Didn't enjoy

TITLE . . . .

AUTHOR . . . .

DATE READ . . . .

THE COVER

RATING   1   2   3   4   5

WHAT DREW ME TO THIS COVER/ WHAT I DIDN'T LOVE ABOUT THIS COVER

. . . .

. . . .

. . . .

WHY I CHOSE THIS BOOK . . . .

. . . .

OTHER BOOKS I HAVE READ OR PLAN TO READ BY THIS AUTHOR
(Check if read already)

◯ . . . .

◯ . . . .

◯ . . . .

◯ . . . .

THE FEELING(S) THIS BOOK EVOKED IN ME . . . .

. . . .

FAVORITE PASSAGE(S) . . . .

. . . .

. . . .

. . . .

. . . .

. . . .

. . . .

DID READING THIS BOOK CHANGE ME IN ANY WAY? . . . .

. . . .

. . . .

WHO WOULD I LIKE TO SHARE THIS BOOK WITH?
WHAT WOULD I HOPE FOR THEM TO TAKE AWAY FROM IT?

. . . .

. . . .

NOT RECOMMENDED? WHY? . . . .

REREAD?   Y   N

RATINGS

WRITING STYLE	Loved it	Just okay	Didn't enjoy
MESSAGE	Loved it	Just okay	Didn't enjoy
READING EXPERIENCE	Loved it	Just okay	Didn't enjoy

TITLE . . . .

AUTHOR . . . .

DATE READ . . . .

THE COVER

RATING   1   2   3   4   5

WHAT DREW ME TO THIS COVER/ WHAT I DIDN'T LOVE ABOUT THIS COVER

. . . .

. . . .

. . . .

WHY I CHOSE THIS BOOK . . . .

. . . .

OTHER BOOKS I HAVE READ OR PLAN TO READ BY THIS AUTHOR
(Check if read already)

○ . . . .

○ . . . .

○ . . . .

○ . . . .

THE FEELING(S) THIS BOOK EVOKED IN ME . . . .

. . . .

FAVORITE PASSAGE(S) . . . .

. . . .

. . . .

. . . .

. . . .

. . . .

. . . .

DID READING THIS BOOK CHANGE ME IN ANY WAY? . . . .

. . . .

. . . .

WHO WOULD I LIKE TO SHARE THIS BOOK WITH?
WHAT WOULD I HOPE FOR THEM TO TAKE AWAY FROM IT?

. . . .

. . . .

NOT RECOMMENDED? WHY? . . . .

REREAD?   Y   N

RATINGS

WRITING STYLE	Loved it	Just okay	Didn't enjoy
MESSAGE	Loved it	Just okay	Didn't enjoy
READING EXPERIENCE	Loved it	Just okay	Didn't enjoy

TITLE . . . .

AUTHOR . . . .

DATE READ . . . .

THE COVER

RATING   1   2   3   4   5

WHAT DREW ME TO THIS COVER/ WHAT I DIDN'T LOVE ABOUT THIS COVER

. . . .

. . . .

. . . .

WHY I CHOSE THIS BOOK . . . .

. . . .

OTHER BOOKS I HAVE READ OR PLAN TO READ BY THIS AUTHOR
(Check if read already)

◯ . . . .

◯ . . . .

◯ . . . .

◯ . . . .

THE FEELING(S) THIS BOOK EVOKED IN ME . . . .

. . . .

FAVORITE PASSAGE(S) . . . .

. . . .

. . . .

. . . .

. . . .

. . . .

. . . .

DID READING THIS BOOK CHANGE ME IN ANY WAY? . . . .

. . . .

. . . .

WHO WOULD I LIKE TO SHARE THIS BOOK WITH?
WHAT WOULD I HOPE FOR THEM TO TAKE AWAY FROM IT?

. . . .

. . . .

NOT RECOMMENDED? WHY? . . . .

REREAD?   Y   N

RATINGS

WRITING STYLE	Loved it	Just okay	Didn't enjoy
MESSAGE	Loved it	Just okay	Didn't enjoy
READING EXPERIENCE	Loved it	Just okay	Didn't enjoy

My Favorite Children's Books

Most book lovers come to love reading as children (though for those who didn't discover the pleasures of reading till later, children's books offer many pleasures, so don't resist just because you're no longer a kid.) The sheer delight of lingering over the pages of a beloved picture book gives way to the page-turning fervor of middle-grade series and the thrill of YA novels. These are my favorite books from childhood as well as the children's books I have discovered more recently:

_____

_____

_____

_____

_____

_____

_____

_____

_____

_____

_____

_____

_____

_____

_____

_____

_____

_____

_____

_____

TITLE . . . .

AUTHOR . . . .

DATE READ . . . .

THE COVER

RATING   1   2   3   4   5

WHAT DREW ME TO THIS COVER/ WHAT I DIDN'T LOVE ABOUT THIS COVER

. . . .

. . . .

. . . .

WHY I CHOSE THIS BOOK . . . .

. . . .

OTHER BOOKS I HAVE READ OR PLAN TO READ BY THIS AUTHOR
(Check if read already)

◯ . . . .

◯ . . . .

◯ . . . .

◯ . . . .

THE FEELING(S) THIS BOOK EVOKED IN ME . . . .

. . . .

FAVORITE PASSAGE(S) . . . .
. . . .
. . . .
. . . .
. . . .
. . . .
. . . .

DID READING THIS BOOK CHANGE ME IN ANY WAY? . . . .
. . . .
. . . .

WHO WOULD I LIKE TO SHARE THIS BOOK WITH?
WHAT WOULD I HOPE FOR THEM TO TAKE AWAY FROM IT?

. . . .
. . . .

NOT RECOMMENDED? WHY? . . . .

REREAD?   Y   N

RATINGS

WRITING STYLE	Loved it	Just okay	Didn't enjoy
MESSAGE	Loved it	Just okay	Didn't enjoy
READING EXPERIENCE	Loved it	Just okay	Didn't enjoy

TITLE . . . .

AUTHOR . . . .

DATE READ . . . .

THE COVER

RATING   1   2   3   4   5

WHAT DREW ME TO THIS COVER/ WHAT I DIDN'T LOVE ABOUT THIS COVER

. . . .

. . . .

. . . .

WHY I CHOSE THIS BOOK . . . .

. . . .

OTHER BOOKS I HAVE READ OR PLAN TO READ BY THIS AUTHOR
(Check if read already)

◯ . . . .

◯ . . . .

◯ . . . .

◯ . . . .

THE FEELING(S) THIS BOOK EVOKED IN ME . . . .

. . . .

FAVORITE PASSAGE(S) . . . .

. . . .

. . . .

. . . .

. . . .

. . . .

. . . .

DID READING THIS BOOK CHANGE ME IN ANY WAY? . . . .

. . . .

. . . .

WHO WOULD I LIKE TO SHARE THIS BOOK WITH?
WHAT WOULD I HOPE FOR THEM TO TAKE AWAY FROM IT?

. . . .

. . . .

NOT RECOMMENDED? WHY? . . . .

REREAD?   Y   N

RATINGS

WRITING STYLE	Loved it	Just okay	Didn't enjoy
MESSAGE	Loved it	Just okay	Didn't enjoy
READING EXPERIENCE	Loved it	Just okay	Didn't enjoy

TITLE . . . .

AUTHOR . . . .

DATE READ . . . .

THE COVER

RATING   1   2   3   4   5

WHAT DREW ME TO THIS COVER/ WHAT I DIDN'T LOVE ABOUT THIS COVER

. . . .

. . . .

. . . .

WHY I CHOSE THIS BOOK . . . .

. . . .

OTHER BOOKS I HAVE READ OR PLAN TO READ BY THIS AUTHOR
(Check if read already)

◯ . . . .

◯ . . . .

◯ . . . .

◯ . . . .

THE FEELING(S) THIS BOOK EVOKED IN ME . . . .

. . . .

FAVORITE PASSAGE(S) . . . .

. . . .

. . . .

. . . .

. . . .

. . . .

. . . .

DID READING THIS BOOK CHANGE ME IN ANY WAY? . . . .

. . . .

. . . .

WHO WOULD I LIKE TO SHARE THIS BOOK WITH?
WHAT WOULD I HOPE FOR THEM TO TAKE AWAY FROM IT?

. . . .

. . . .

NOT RECOMMENDED? WHY? . . . .

REREAD?   Y   N

RATINGS

WRITING STYLE	Loved it	Just okay	Didn't enjoy
MESSAGE	Loved it	Just okay	Didn't enjoy
READING EXPERIENCE	Loved it	Just okay	Didn't enjoy

TITLE . . . .

AUTHOR . . . .

DATE READ . . . .

THE COVER

RATING   1   2   3   4   5

WHAT DREW ME TO THIS COVER/ WHAT I DIDN'T LOVE ABOUT THIS COVER

. . . .

. . . .

. . . .

WHY I CHOSE THIS BOOK . . . .

. . . .

OTHER BOOKS I HAVE READ OR PLAN TO READ BY THIS AUTHOR
(Check if read already)

◯ . . . .

◯ . . . .

◯ . . . .

◯ . . . .

THE FEELING(S) THIS BOOK EVOKED IN ME . . . .

. . . .

FAVORITE PASSAGE(S) . . . .
. . . .
. . . .
. . . .
. . . .
. . . .
. . . .

DID READING THIS BOOK CHANGE ME IN ANY WAY? . . . .
. . . .
. . . .

WHO WOULD I LIKE TO SHARE THIS BOOK WITH?
WHAT WOULD I HOPE FOR THEM TO TAKE AWAY FROM IT?

. . . .
. . . .

NOT RECOMMENDED? WHY? . . . .

REREAD?   Y   N

RATINGS

WRITING STYLE	Loved it	Just okay	Didn't enjoy
MESSAGE	Loved it	Just okay	Didn't enjoy
READING EXPERIENCE	Loved it	Just okay	Didn't enjoy

Genre Hound: My Favorite Genre

What type of book do you find yourself returning to over and over? Perhaps you have a collection of engrossing historical novels, an obsession with epic fantasy, or shelves overflowing with the promise of self-help. Or perhaps there is a new favorite genre that you're just beginning to explore. My favorites:

_____

_____

_____

_____

_____

_____

_____

_____

_____

_____

_____

_____

_____

_____

_____

_____

_____

_____

My Reading Notes

"It wasn't until I started reading and found books they wouldn't let us read in school that I discovered you could be insane and happy and have a good life without being like everybody else."

—John Waters, *The Tenacity of the Cockroach*

"You think your pain and your heartbreak are unprecedented in the history of the world, but then you read. It was Dostoevsky and Dickens who taught me that the things that tormented me most were the very things that connected me with all the people who were alive, or who had ever been alive."

—James Baldwin

Printed in China

SPRUCE BOOKS with colophon is a registered trademark of Penguin Random House LLC

25 24 23 22 21   9 8 7 6 5 4 3 2 1

Editor: Sharyn Rosart
Production editor: Jill Saginario
Designer: Alison Keefe
Illustrations: Alison Keefe

ISBN: 978-1-63217-422-2

Spruce Books, a Sasquatch Books Imprint
1904 Third Avenue, Suite 710
Seattle, WA 98101

SasquatchBooks.com

"So Matilda's strong young mind continued to
grow, nurtured by the voices of all those authors who
had sent their books out into the world like ships
on the sea. These books gave Matilda a hopeful and
comforting message: You are not alone."

–Roald Dahl